THE OLD HUMANITIES
AND
THE NEW SCIENCE

First published 1920
This edition published by Lector House in 2024

ISBN: 978-93-6138-871-2
Edition copyright © 2024 by Lector House LLP
All rights reserved under the International Copyright Conventions.

Every possible effort has been made to ensure that the information contained in this book is accurate at the time of going to press and the publisher cannot accept responsibility for any errors or omissions, however caused, in this unabridged, slightly corrected republication of the text of the first edition. No responsibility for loss or damage occasioned to any person, acting or refraining from action, as a result of the material in this publication can be accepted by the publisher. The publisher is not associated with any product or vendor mentioned in the book. The contents of this work are intended to further general scientific research, understanding and discussion, only. Readers should consult with a specialist, where appropriate.

No part of this publication may be reproduced, stored in a retrieval system, or transmitted, in any form, or by any means, electronic, mechanical, photocopying or otherwise, without the prior permission of the publisher.

Lector House LLP
Registered Office: H. No. 96, Block C, Tomar Colony,
Burari, Delhi – 110084, India
info@lectorhouse.com
www.lectorhouse.com

THE OLD HUMANITIES AND THE NEW SCIENCE

WILLIAM OSLER,
HARVEY CUSHING

2024

LECTOR HOUSE
LECTOR HOUSE LLP

THE OLD HUMANITIES
AND
THE NEW SCIENCE

PRESIDENTIAL ADDRESS TO THE CLASSICAL ASSOCIATION MAY 16, 1919

BY

SIR WILLIAM OSLER, BT., M.D., F.R.S.

WITH INTRODUCTION BY
HARVEY CUSHING, M.D.

Contents

Introduction

In writing a prefatory note to an American reprint of this notable address there are three things to consider—the writer, his subject, and the occasion. The greatly beloved author had a multitude of friends in all lands, and far abler pens have written much concerning him during the past twelve months. The subject is one of no less moment on this side of the Atlantic than to those in older countries who concern themselves with scholarship and education, though here the classicists are having a particularly hard struggle to retain in our academies, schools, and colleges a proper footing for the ancient languages and learning termed "the humanities." The circumstances under which the address was given are less familiar in this country than the author and his subject, for we as yet have no corresponding organization, or at least none with such an ambitious programme. Consequently it is appropriate that this note should dwell chiefly upon the occasion.

The Classical Association, composed of a large body of university men, teachers, and schoolmasters, with local branches in several places in Great Britain and her colonies, was established in 1904 with this object:

> To promote the development and maintain the well-being of classical studies and in particular:

> (a) To impress upon public opinion the claim of such studies to an eminent place in the national scheme of education;

> (b) To improve the practice of classical teaching by free discussion of its scope and methods;

> (c) To encourage investigation and call attention to new discoveries;

> (d) To create opportunities for friendly intercourse and co-operation among all lovers of classical learning in this country.

That Sir William Osler should have been chosen to preside over such an assembly of British scholars is no matter for surprise, for though a humanist in the broad sense of the term as a student of human affairs and human nature, rather than of Latin and Greek, he at the same time was a wide reader with a "relish for knowledge," successful not only in its quest in many fields beyond that of his chosen profession, but particularly so in his ability to hand his literary gleanings on to others in a new and attractive form. Nevertheless, the presidency of the Classical Association, considering the avowed objects of this body, was a most signal honour in view of his reputation primarily as a scientist and teacher of medicine.

His immediate predecessor, the Professor of Greek at Christ Church, opened his presidential address of the year before with these words:

> It is the general custom of this Association to choose as its President alternately a classical scholar and a man of wide eminence outside the classics. Next year you are to have a man of science, a great physician who is also famous in the world of learning and literature. Last year you had a statesman, who, though a statesman, is also a great scholar and man of letters, a sage and counsellor in the antique mould, of world-wide fame and unique influence.

Thus, though in himself sufficiently representative of humanistic culture, Osler was in this strict sense an alternate, and among the fourteen earlier Presidents of the Association three had like himself been Fellows of the Royal Society, which long since had abandoned even the pretence of concerning itself with classical studies which had been the very basis of the Revival of Learning.

The list of Presidents since the foundation of the Association may be a matter of interest to those in this country who may not have been aware of the existence and purposes of this organization of British scholars:

1904. The Right Hon. Sir R. H. Collins, M.A., LL.D., D.C.L., Master of the Rolls.

1905. The Right Hon. the Earl of Halsbury, D.C.L., F.R.S., Lord Chancellor.

1906. The Right Hon. Lord Curzon of Kedleston, G.C.S.I., G.C.I.E., D.C.L., F.R.S.

1907. S. H. Butcher, Esq., M.P., Litt.D., D.Litt., LL.D.

1908. The Right Hon. H. H. Asquith, M.P., K.C., D.C.L., Prime Minister.

1909. The Right Hon. the Earl of Cromer, G.C.B., O.M., K.C.S.I., LL.D.

1910. Sir Archibald Geikie, K.C.B., D.C.L., LL.D., Ph.D., President of the Royal Society.

1911. The Right Rev. Edward Lee Hicks, D.D., Lord Bishop of Lincoln.

1912. The Very Rev. Henry Montagu Butler, D.D., D.C.L., LL.D., Master of Trinity College, Cambridge.

1913. Sir Frederic G. Kenyon, K.C.B., D.Litt., F.B.A., Head of the British Museum.

1914. Professor William Ridgeway, Litt.D., LL.D., Sc.D., F.B.A., Disney Professor of Archæology, Cambridge.

1915. Sir W. B. Richmond, K.C.B., R.A., D.C.L.

1916. The Right Hon. Viscount Bryce, O.M., D.C.L., LL.D., P.B.A., F.R.S.

1917.   Professor Gilbert Murray, LL.D., D.Litt., F.B.A., F.R.S.L., Christ Church, Oxford.

As reported in the Annual Proceedings of the Association, Professor Murray at the meeting in 1918, in nominating his successor, spoke of him as a man, "who is not only one of the most eminent physicians in the world, but represents in a peculiar way the learned physician who was one of the marked characters of the seventeenth and eighteenth centuries, and stands for a type of culture which the Classical Association does not wish to see die out of the world—the culture of a man who, while devoting himself to his special science, keeps nevertheless a broad basis of interest in letters of all kinds."

In seconding this proposal, Sir Frederic Kenyon pointed out that it had come at a very appropriate time in the work of the Association, for: "During this last year our main activity has been directed towards getting representatives of Natural Science and of the Humanities to work together, on the principle that those subjects never should be in conflict with one another, but merely in friendly competition. Both are equally essential for a liberal education. It is a continuation and a symbol of that policy that we should ask Sir William Osler to become our President, and that he should have accepted cordially and readily, as he did. He is eminent as a man of science, is President of the Bibliographical Society, and represents scholarship in medicine in its best form."

It is quite possible that these last remarks may have suggested to the succeeding President an appropriate topic for his address, for he told the writer a few months later that he planned to talk on Science and the Humanities. He was already turning the matter over in his mind, but where he found time or inclination to write the address it is difficult to imagine.

Staggered by the loss of his son, an only child, who had fallen in action near St. Julien during the Passchendaele battles in September the year before, his days occupied with a succession of duties in connection with the war, his household filled as always with friends and visitors innumerable, and every young American or Canadian in service in England gravitating there, eager above all things to further the progress of the elaborate catalogue of his unique and valuable collection of books, he nevertheless set himself to prepare this, one of his most brilliant and what proved to be his last formal address.

The meeting of the Association was to be held in Oxford, the bed-rock of classical learning—the only place, it seems, where the word "humanism" in its narrow sense still survives in modern university terminology as that part of the curriculum known as *Litteræ Humaniores*. As was characteristic of his methods, the mere address itself did not suffice, but he prepared for the occasion in other ways. Thus he collected from the various Oxford colleges and placed on exhibition an array of historical objects illustrating the important part Oxford had once played in science and natural philosophy in days antedating the Royal Society which had its seeds of origin there. In addition, and as a possible offset to this, he exhibited from his own collection of books those volumes which constituted in their original editions the outstanding classics in Science and Medicine. A small pamphlet concerning them reads as follows:

> Faced with a bewildering variety and ever-increasing literature, how is the hard-pressed student to learn—
>
> 1. The evolution of knowledge in any subject;
>
> 2. The life and work of the men who made the original contributions?

So far as concerns Science and Medicine, an attempt is made to answer the question by the collection of a Bibliotheca Prima, examples from which are here shown. The idea is to have in a comparatively small number of works the essential literature grouped about the men of the first rank, arranged in chronological order.

I have put out the *editiones principes* of twenty of such works. The fundamental contribution may be represented by a great Aldine edition, *e.g.* Aristotle, by the brief communication such as that of Darwin and Wallace in the Proceedings of the Linnean Society, 1858, or by a three-page pamphlet of Roentgen. From the card lists of Galen, Hippocrates, Vesalius, and Harvey, those interested will see the aim and scope of the collection.

The works on exhibition are:

Plato	1513	Averrhoes	1473
Hippocrates	1526	Copernicus	1543
Aristotle	1495-98	Vesalius	1543
Theophrastus	1483	Agricola	1556
Galen	1525	Gilbert	1600
Dioscorides	1499	Bacon	1620
Celsus	1478	Galileo	1632
Plotinus	1492	Harvey	1628
Rhazes	1476	Descartes	1637
Avicenna	1486 (not ed. pr.)	Newton	1687

Though it is hardly pertinent to this introductory note, the temptation is strong to dwell further on the treasures of his library. These mentioned above were but samples from the Bibliotheca Prima, and the superb collection, with copious notes on each separate item, is further subdivided into some seven sections—Bibliotheca Secunda, historica, biographica, literaria, the incunabulas, and so on.

He was for seven years President of the Bibliographical Society and as great a lover of books as of men, but it should be borne in mind that his library was being collected and catalogued, not as a series of treasures by reason of their rarity, but were regarded as instruments for the advancement of knowledge, and with this end in view the collection was bequeathed to McGill University.

By good fortune, letters which give interesting descriptions of the effect of the address have been received from two distinguished members of Sir William's audience, one of them an eminent classical scholar, the other an eminent scientist. Sir Frederic Kenyon writes that:

The delivery of Sir William Osler's address was a very memorable occasion. As can be seen by those who read it, it was full of learning, of humour, of feeling, of eloquence, and it contained suggestions of real weight with regard to the interconnection of science and the humanities. But it gained much in delivery from the personality of the speaker. No one could hear it without being impressed by his width of outlook, by his easy mastery of great tracts of literature and learning, by his all-embracing humanity in the widest sense of the term. I hope it made many students of science anxious to extend their knowledge of classical literature; I know it made one student of the classics wish that he had a wider knowledge of natural science. Osler himself was a well-nigh perfect example of the union of science and the humanities, which to some of us is the ideal of educational progress; and his address embodied the whole spirit of this ideal.

Professor William H. Welch has given the following account:

Most fortunately for me my last visit to the Oslers' in Oxford happened to be on Friday, May 16, 1919, when Osler delivered his presidential address before the Classical Association.

Of the many honours which came to Osler few gave him so great pleasure, as well as surprise, as his election to the presidency of the British Classical Association. This was a recognition, not merely of his sympathetic interest in classical studies and intimate association with classical scholars, but also of his mastery of certain phases of the subject, especially the bibliographical and historical sides, and the relation of the work and thought of classical antiquity to the development of medicine, science, and culture. There have been physicians, especially in England, well known for their attainments as classical scholars, but I am not aware that since Linacre there has come to a member of the medical profession distinction in this field comparable to Osler's election to the presidency of the British Classical

Association.

Osler told me that he had never given so much time and thought to the preparation of an address as he did to this one. The occasion and the whole setting were to me most interesting and impressive. At noon the audience of distinguished scholars and guests assembled in the "Divinity Room," the most beautiful assembly room in Oxford. At one end of the hall the Vice-Chancellor of the University presided and halfway down one of the sides was the high seat of the orator. The distinguished company, the brightly coloured academic gowns and hoods, the traditional ceremonies for such an occasion in Oxford, the figure of Osler himself, the charm and interest of the address and its cordial appreciation and reception by the audience, all combined to make a scene of brilliancy and delight which I shall always carry in my memory.

At the close of the address the vote of thanks was moved by Sir Herbert Warren, the President of Magdalen College, who described Osler as the modern Galen, and was seconded by Sir John Barran, the member of Parliament from Leeds, in felicitous words of discriminating praise of the President's address. The audience responded most enthusiastically.

I shall never forget the hour which I spent with Osler just before the address, in inspecting the wonderful collection of scientific instruments of historical interest which Mr. Gunther had assembled at Osler's request from the various colleges at Oxford, especially from Merton, the old home of science. An interesting descriptive catalogue of the collection had been prepared. With what delight Osler showed me and told me the histories and associations of the astrolabes, armillary spheres, orreries, telescopes, lenses, microscopes, books, etc., which he had caused to be gathered together in connection with the meeting of the Classical Association! You will recognize a characteristic touch and thought of Osler in arranging for such an original exhibit to interest a meeting of scholars.

When not long after the address I said good-bye to Osler I little thought that it was to be our final parting, but I rejoice to have been with him then and to remember him as I saw him last on that triumphal day.

Thus, though from first to last his heart was wrapped up in his profession and its science, his mind was open to other things, and his confession that the *Religio Medici* was the second book he ever purchased and that the particular copy had always remained at his bedside is not without significance. He lived to prove himself, not only a worthy disciple of those scholars of the Renascence who interested themselves in natural philosophy, but also of those who were devotees of the ancient languages and literature. But Sir William Osler was a man first—a physician and scholar afterward; and beneath his high spirits, his love of fun, lay an infinite compassion and tenderness toward his humankind. "Write me as one who loves his fellow-men." And upon few men has such a measure of admiration, affection, and love been bestowed in return. These things he bore without pride, as he bore his great success in life with humility.

On July 12, 1919, less than two months after the address was delivered, he attained his seventieth year, and was presented with two volumes containing sixty-seven original "Contributions to Medical and Biological Research" written in his honour. In addition to this, tributes were showered upon him from all sides, and his work, character, and accomplishments became the subject of papers innumerable. It was an extraordinary outburst, one of those exceptional occurrences when people do not wait for the passing—in this case so near at hand—to say, what is in their hearts to say, of the life of a friend. A brief characterization of him from one of the most eminent of British scholars was quoted early in this note, and it may be fitting to close with some lines by the dean of American classical scholars, Basil L. Gildersleeve, written for what proved to be his last birthday:

ON A PORTRAIT OF SIR WILLIAM OSLER, BART.

William the Fowler, Guillaume l'Oiseleur!
I love to call him thus, and when I scan

The counterfeit presentment of the man,
I feel his net, I hear his arrows whir.
Make at the homely surname no demur,
Nor on a nomination lay a ban
With which a line of sovran lords began,
Henry the Fowler was first Emperor.

Asclepius was Apollo's chosen son,
But to that son he never lent his bow,
Nor did Hephæstus teach to forge his net;
Both secrets hath Imperial Osler won.
His winged words straight to their quarry go.
All hearts are holden by his meshes yet.

HARVEY CUSHING

Brookline
  February 18, 1920

THE OLD HUMANITIES
AND
THE NEW SCIENCE

I

Early in the sixteenth century a literary joke sent inextinguishable laughter through the learned circles of Europe. The *Epistolæ Obscurorum Virorum* is great literature, to which I refer for two reasons—its standard is an exact gauge of my scholarship, and had *Magister Nostrandus Ortuinus Gratius* of Cologne, to whom most of the letters are addressed, been asked to join that wicked Erfurt Circle, he could not have been more surprised than I was to receive a gracious invitation to preside over this gathering of British scholars. I felt to have been sailing under false colours to have ever, by pen or tongue, suggested the possession of even the traditional small Latin and less Greek. Relieved by the assurance that in alternate years the qualification of your President was an interest in education and literature, I gladly accepted, not, however, without such anticipatory qualms as afflict an amateur at the thought of addressing a body of experts. Not an educated man in the Oxford sense, yet faint memories of the classics linger—the result of ten years of such study as lads of my generation pursued, memories best expressed in Tom Hood's lines:

> "The weary tasks I used to con!
> The hopeless leaves I wept upon!
> Most fruitless leaves to me!"

In a life of teaching and practice, a mere picker-up of learning's crumbs is made to realize the value of the humanities in science not less than in general culture.

To have a Professor of Medicine in this Chair gives to the Oxford meeting an appropriate renaissance—shall we say mediæval?—flavour, and one may be pardoned the regret that the meeting is not being held in May, 1519, to have had the pleasure of listening to an address from a real Oxford scholar-physician, an early teacher of Greek in this University, and the founder of the Royal College of Physicians, whose *Rudimenta Grammatices* and *De Emendata Structura Latini Sermonis* upheld for a generation, on the Continent at least, the reputation of English scholarship. These noble walls, themselves an audience—indeed, most appreciative of audiences—have storied memories of Linacre's voice, and the basis of the keen judgment of Erasmus may have been formed by intercourse with him in this very school. In those happy days, to know Hippocrates and Galen was to know disease and to be qualified to practise; and my profession looks back in grateful admiration to such great medical humanists as Linacre and Caius and Rabelais. Nor can I claim to speak for pure science, some salt of which remains from early association, and from a lifelong attempt to correlate with art a science which makes medicine, I was going to say the only—but it is more civil to say the most—progressive of the learned professions.

To have lived right through an epoch, matched only by two in the story of the race, to have shared in its long struggle, to have witnessed its final victory (and in my own case, to be left I trust with wit enough to realize its significance)—to have done this has been a wonderful privilege. To have outgrown age-old theories of man and of nature, to have seen west separated from east in the tangled skein of human thought, to have lived in a world re-making—these are among the thrills and triumphs of the Victorian of my generation. To a childhood and youth came echoes of the controversy that Aristarchus began, Copernicus continued, and Darwin ended, that put the microcosm into line with the macrocosm, and for the golden age of Eden substituted the *tellus dura* of Lucretius. Think of the Cimmerian darkness out of which our generation has, at any rate, blazed a path! Picture the mental state of a community which could produce "Omphalos: An Attempt to untie the Geological Knot"![1] I heard warm clerical discussions on its main thesis, that the fossils were put into the earth's strata to test men's faith in the Mosaic account of the creation, and our Professor of Natural Theology lectured seriously upon it! The intellectual unrest of those days wrapped many in that "dyvine cloude of unknowynge," by which happy

---

[1] By the distinguished naturalist Philip Henry Gosse.

phrase Brother Herp designates mediæval mysticism; and not a bad thing for a young man to live through, as sufficient infection usually remains to enable him to understand, if not to sympathize with, mental states alien or even hostile.

An Age of Force followed the final subjugation of Nature. The dynamo replaced the steam-engine, radiant energy revealed the hidden secrets of matter, to the conquest of the earth was added the control of the air and the mastery of the deep. Nor was it only an Age of Force. Never before had man done so much for his brother, the victory over the powers of Nature meant also glorious victories of peace; pestilences were checked, the cry of the poor became articulate, and to help the life of the submerged half became a sacred duty of the other. How full we were of the pride of life! In 1910 at Edinburgh I ended an address on "Man's Redemption of Man" with the well-known lines of Shelley beginning, "Happiness and Science dawn though late upon the earth." And now, having survived the greatest war in history, and a great victory, with the wreckage of mediæval autonomy to clear up, our fears are lest we may fail to control the fretful forces of Caliban, and our hopes are to rebuild Jerusalem in this green and pleasant land.

Never before in its long evolution has the race realized its full capacity. Our fathers have told us, and we ourselves have known, of glorious sacrifices; but the past four years have exhausted in every direction the possibilities of human effort. And, as usual, among the nations the chief burden has fallen on that weary Titan, the Motherland,

> "Bearing on shoulders immense,
> Atlantean, the load
> Well-nigh not to be borne
> Of the too vast orb of her fate."

Not alone did she furnish the sinews of war, but she developed a spirit that made defeat impossible.

No wonder war has advocates, to plead the heroic clash of ideals, the purging of a nation's dross in the fire of suffering and sacrifice, and the welding in one great purpose of a scattered people. Even Montaigne, sanest of men, called it "the greatest and most magnificent of human actions"; and the glamours of its pride, pomp, and circumstance still captivate. But there are other sides which we should face without shrinking. Why dwell on the horrors such as we doctors and nurses have had to see? Enough to say that war blasts the soul, and in this great conflict the finer sense of humanity has been shocked to paralysis by the helplessness of our civilization and the futility of our religion to stem a wave of primitive barbarism. Black as are the written and unwritten pages of history, the concentrated and prolonged martyrdom surpasses anything man has yet had to endure. What a shock to the proud and mealy-mouthed Victorian who had begun to trust that Love was creation's final law, forgetting that Egypt and Babylon are our contemporaries and of yesterday in comparison with the hundreds of thousands of years since the cave-dwellers left their records on walls and bones. In the mystic shadow of the Golden Bough, and swayed by the emotions of our savage ancestors, we stand aghast at the revelation of the depth and ferocity of primal passions which reveal the unchangeableness of human nature.

When the wild beast of Plato's dream becomes a waking reality, and a herd-emotion of hate sweeps a nation off its feet, the desolation that follows is wider than that in France and Belgium, wider even than the desolation of grief, and something worse—the hardened heart, the lie in the soul—so graphically described in Book II of the "Republic"—that forces us to do accursed things, and even to defend them! I refer to it because, as professors, we have been accused of sinning against the light. Of course we have. Over us, too, the wave swept, but I protest against the selection of us for special blame. The other day, in an address on "The Comradeship of Letters" at Turin, President Wilson is reported to have said: "It is one of the great griefs of this war that the universities of the Central Empires used the thoughts of science to destroy mankind; it is the duty of the universities of these states to redeem science from this disgrace and to show that the pulse of humanity beats in the classroom, and that there are sought out not the secrets of death but the secrets of life." A pious and worthy wish! But once in war a nation mobilizes every energy, and to say that science has been prostituted in discovering means of butchery is to misunderstand the situation. Slaughter, wholesale and unrestricted, is what is sought, and to accomplish this the discoveries of the sainted Faraday and of the gentle Dalton are utilized to the full, and to their several nations scientific men render this service freely, if not gladly. That the mental attitude engendered by science is apt to lead to a gross materialism is a vulgar error. Scientific men, in mufti or in uniform, are not more brutal than their fellows, and the utilization of their discoveries in warfare should not be a greater reproach to them than is our joyous acceptance of their success.

What a change of heart after the appalling experience of the first gassing in 1915! Nothing more piteously horrible than the sufferings of the victims has ever been seen in warfare.[2] Surely we could not sink to such barbarity! Is thy servant a dog? But martial expediency soon compelled the Allies to enlist the resources of chemistry; the instruction of our enemies was soon bettered, and before the Armistice there were developments in technique and destructive force that would have delighted Nisroch, who first invented aerial "machinations to plague the sons of men." A group of medical men representing the chief universities and medical bodies of the United Kingdom was innocent enough to suggest that such an unclean weapon— the use of lethal gases, "condemning its victims to death by long-drawn-out torture," and with infinite possibilities for its further development—should be forever abolished. "Steeped in folly by theories and prepossessions," failure to read the "lessons of war which should have sufficed to convince a beetle"—such were among the newspaper comments; and in other ways we were given to understand that our interference in such matters was most untimely. All the same, it is gratifying to see that the suggestion has been adopted at the Peace Congress.

With what a howl of righteous indignation the slaughter of our innocent women and children by the bombing of open towns was received! It was a dirty and bloody business, worthy of the Oxydracians by means of Levin-bolts and Thunders and more horrible, more frightful, more diabolical, maiming, breaking, tearing, and slaying more folk and confounding men's senses and throwing down more walls than would a hundred thunderbolts.[3]

Against reprisals there was at first a strong feeling. Early in 1916 I wrote to the "Times": "The cry for reprisals illustrates the exquisitely hellish state of mind into which war plunges even sensible men. Not a pacifist, but a 'last-ditcher,' yet I refuse to believe that as a nation, how bitter soever the

[2] I am sorry to have seen Sargent's picture "Gassed" in this year's Academy. It haunts the mind like a nightmare.

[3] Rabelais, Book IV, ch. LXI.

provocation, we shall stain our hands in the blood of the innocent. In this matter let us be free from bloodguiltiness, and let not the undying reproach of humanity rest on us as on the Germans." Two years changed me into an ordinary barbarian. A detailed tally of civilians killed by our airmen has not, I believe, been published, but the total figures quoted are not far behind the German.

Could a poll have been taken a week before the Armistice as to the moral justification of the bombing of Berlin—for which we were ready—how we should have howled at the proposer of any doubt! And many Jonahs were displeased that a city greater than Nineveh, with more than the threescore and ten thousand who knew not the right hand from the left, had been spared. We may deplore the necessity and lament, as did a certain great personage:

> "... Yet public reason just—
> Honour and empire with revenge enlarged
> ... compels me now
> To do what else, though damned, I should abhor."

All the same, we considered ourselves "Christians of the best edition, all picked and culled," and the churches remained open, prayers rose to Jehovah, many of whose priests—even his bishops!—were in khaki, and quit themselves like men—yes, and scores died the death of heroes! Into such hells of inconsistency does war plunge the best of us!

Learning—new or old—seems a vain thing to save a nation, but possibly, as a set-off, science, as represented by cellulose and sulphuric acid, may yet prove the best bulwark of civilization! In his "History of the Origin of Medicine,"[4] Lettsom maintains that the invention of firearms has done more to prevent the destruction of the human species than any other discovery; he says: "Invention and discernment of mind have made it possible to reverse the ancient maxim that strength has always prevailed over wisdom." Science alone may prevent a repetition of the story of Egypt, of Babylonia, of Greece, and of Rome. The suggestion seems brazen effrontery when we have not even given the world the equivalent of the *Pax Romana*! Ah! what a picture of self-satisfied happiness in Plutarch! One envies that placid life in the midst of the only great peace the world

---

[4] 1778, p. 30.

has known, spanning a period of more than two hundred years. And he could say, "No tumults, no civil sedition, no tyrannies, no pestilences nor calamities depopulating Greece, no epidemic disease needing powerful and choice drugs and medicines"; though as a Delphic priest there is a pathetic lament that the Pythian priestess has now only commonplace questions to deal with.[5] Surely those cultivated men of his circle must have felt that their house could never be removed. Has Science reached such control over Nature that she will enable our civilization to escape the law of the Ephesian, written on all known records—*panta rei*? Perhaps so, now that material civilization is world-wide; cataclysmic forces, powerful enough in centres of origin, may weaken as they pass out in circles. Let this be our hope in the present crisis. At any rate, in the free democracies in which Demos with safety says "*L'État c'est moi*," it has yet to be determined whether Science, as the embodiment of a mechanical force, can rule without invoking ruin. Two things are clear: there must be a very different civilization or there will be no civilization at all; and the other is that neither the old religion combined with the old learning, nor both with the new science, suffice to save a nation bent on self-destruction. The suicide of Germany, the outstanding fact of the war, followed an outburst of national megalomania. For she had religion—it may shock some of you to hear! I mean the people, not the writers or the thinkers, but the people for whom Luther lived and Huss died. Of the two devotional ceremonies which stand supreme in my memory, one was a service in the Dom, Berlin, in which "not the great nor well bespoke, but the mere uncounted folk" sang Luther's great hymn "*Ein' feste Burg ist unser Gott.*"[6] With the Humanities Germany never broke, and the proportion of students in her schools and universities who studied Greek and Latin has been higher than in any other country. You know better than I the innumerable classical studies of her scholars. In classical learning relating to science and medicine she simply had the field; for one scholar in other countries she had a dozen, and the monopoly of journals relating to the history of these subjects. And she had science, and led the world in the application of the products of the laboratory to the uses of every-day life—in commerce, in the arts, and in war. Withal, like Jeshurun, she waxed fat; and did ever such pride go before such destruction? What a tragedy that the

[5] "Why the Pythian Priestess," etc. (Plutarch's *Morals*, vol. III, p. 100, Goodwin's edition).

[6] And the other, how different! The crowded Blue Mosque of Cairo, and the crowded streets with the thousands of kneeling Moslems awaiting the cry of the muezzin from the tower.

successors of Virchow and Traube and Helmholtz and Billroth should have made her a byword among the nations! "Lilies that fester smell far worse than weeds!"

II

So much preliminary to the business before us, to meet changed conditions as practical men, with the reinforcement born of hope or with the strong resolution of despair.

For what does this Association stand? What are these classical interests that you represent? Take a familiar simile. By a very simple trick, you remember, did Empedocles give Menippus in the moon-halt—the first stage of his memorable trip—such long and clear vision that he saw the tribes of men like a nest of ants, a seething mass going to and fro at their different tasks. Of the function of the classical members in this myrmecic community there can be no question. Neither warriors, nor slaves, nor neuters, you live in a well-protected social environment, heretofore free from enemies, and have been well taken care of. I hate to speak of you as larvæ, but as such you perform a duty of the greatest import in this trophidium stage of your existence. Let me explain. From earliest days much attention has been paid by naturalists to the incredible affection "—incredible στοργή," Swammerdam calls it—which ants display in feeding, licking, and attending the larvæ. Disturb a nest, and the chief care is to take them to a place of safety. This attention is what our symphilic community—to use a biological term— bestows on you. So intensely altruistic, apparently, is this behaviour, that for the very word "στοργή," which expresses the tenderest of all feelings, there is a difficulty in finding an equivalent; indeed, Gilbert White used it almost as an English word. The truth is really very different.

It has been shown that the nursing function—or instinct—is really trophallactic. In the case of the ant the nurse places the larva on its back, and the broad ventral surface serves as a trough for the food, often predigested.

The skill and devotion with which this is done are among the wonders in the life of the insect to which moralists have never tired of urging a visit. But listen to the sequel! The larva is provided with a pair of rich honey-bags in the shape of salivary glands, big exudatoria from which is discharged an ambrosia greedily lapped up by the nurse, who with this considers herself well paid for her care. In the same manner, when the assiduous V.A.D. wasp distributes food to the larvæ, the heads of which eagerly protrude from their cells, she must be paid by a draught of nectar from their exudatoria, while if it is not forthcoming the wasp seizes the head of the larva in her mandibles and jams it back into its cell and compels it to pay up. The lazy males will play the same game and even steal the much-sought liquid without any compensatory gift of nourishment.[7]

What does the community at large, so careful of your comforts, expect from you? Surely the honey-dew and the milk of paradise secreted from your classical exudatoria, which we lap up greedily in recensions, monographs, commentaries, histories, translations, and brochures. Among academic larvæ you have for centuries absorbed the almost undivided interest of the nest, and not without reason, for the very life of the workers depends on the hormones you secrete. Though small in number, your group has an enormous kinetic value, like our endocrine organs. For man's body, too, is a humming hive of working cells, each with its specific function, all under central control of the brain and heart, and all dependent on materials called hormones (secreted by small, even insignificant-looking structures) which lubricate the wheels of life. For example, remove the thyroid gland just below the Adam's apple, and you deprive man of the lubricants which enable his thought-engines to work—it is as if you cut off the oil-supply of a motor—and gradually the stored acquisitions of his mind cease to be available, and within a year he sinks into dementia. The normal processes of the skin cease, the hair falls, the features bloat, and the paragon of animals is transformed into a shapeless caricature of humanity. These essential lubricators, of which a number are now known, are called hormones—you will recognize from its derivation how appropriate is the term.

Now, the men of your guild secrete materials which do for society at large what the thyroid gland does for the individual. The Humanities are the hormones. Our friend Mr. P. S. Allen read before this Association a most

---

[7] Professor Wheeler in *Proceedings of Amer. Phil. Soc.*, vol. LVII, no. 4, 1918.

suggestive paper on the historical evolution of the word "Humanism." I like to think of the pleasant-flavoured word as embracing all the knowledge of the ancient classical world—what man knew of nature as well as what he knew of himself. Let us see what this university means by the *Literæ Humaniores*. The "Greats" papers for the past decade make interesting study. With singular uniformity there is diversity enough to bear high tribute to the ingenuity of the examiners. But, comparing the subjects in 1918 with those in the first printed papers of the school in 1831, one is surprised to find them the same—practically no change in the eighty-seven years! Compare them, again, with the subjects given in John Napleton's "Considerations" in 1773—no change! and with the help of Rashdall we may trace the story of the studies in arts, only to find that as far back as 1267, with different names sometimes, they have been through all the centuries essentially the same—Greek and Latin authors, logic, rhetoric, grammar, and the philosophies, natural, moral, and metaphysical—practically the seven liberal arts for which, as you may see by the names over the doors, Bodley's building provided accommodation. Why this invariableness in an ever-turning world? One of the marvels, so commonplace that it has ceased to be marvellous, is the deep rooting of our civilization in the soil of Greece and Rome—much of our dogmatic religion, practically all the philosophies, the models of our literature, the ideals of our democratic freedom, the fine and the technical arts, the fundamentals of science, and the basis of our law. The Humanities bring the student into contact with the master minds who gave us these things—with the dead who never die, with those immortal lives "not of now nor of yesterday, but which always were."

As true to-day as in the fifth century B.C. the name of Hellas stands no longer for the name of a race, but as the name of knowledge; or, as more tersely put by Maine, "Except the blind forces of Nature, nothing moves [intellectually, he means] in this world that is not Greek in origin." Man's anabasis from the old priest-ridden civilizations of the East began when "the light of reason lighted up all things," with which saying Anaxagoras expressed our modern outlook on life.

The Humanities have been a subject of criticism in two directions. Their overwhelming prominence, it is claimed, prevents the development of learning in other and more useful directions; and the method of teaching is said to be antiquated and out of touch with the present needs. They control the academic life of Oxford. An analysis of the Register for 1919 shows that of the 257 men comprising the Heads and Fellows of the twenty-three colleges (including St. Edmund's Hall), only fifty-one are scientific, including the mathematicians.

It is not very polite, perhaps, to suggest that as transmitters and interpreters they should not bulk quite so large in a modern university. 'Twas all very well

> "... in days when wits were fresh and clear
> And life ran gaily as the sparkling Thames—"

in those happy days when it was felt that all knowledge had been garnered by those divine men of old time, that there was nothing left but to enjoy the good things harvested by such universal providers as Isidore, Rabanus Maurus, and Vincent of Beauvais, and those stronger dishes served by such artists as Albertus Magnus and St. Thomas Aquinas—delicious blends of such skill that only the palate of an Apicius could separate Greek, Patristic, and Arabian savours.

It is not the dominance, but the unequal dominance that is a cause of just complaint. As to methods of teaching—by their fruits ye shall know them. The product of "Greats" needs no description in this place. Many deny the art to find the mind's construction in the face, but surely not the possibility of diagnosing at a glance a "first in Greats"! Only in him is seen that altogether superior expression, that self-consciousness of having reached life's goal, of having, in that pickled sentence of Dean Gaisford's Christmas sermon, done something "that not only elevates above the common herd, but leads not unfrequently to positions of considerable emolument." "Many are the wand-bearers, few are the mystics," and a system should not be judged by the exceptions. As a discipline of the mind for the few, the system should not be touched, and we should be ready to sacrifice a holocaust of undergraduates every year to produce in each generation a scholar of the type of, say, Ingram Bywater. 'Tis Nature's method—does it not cost some thousands of eggs and fry to produce one salmon?

But the average man, not of scholar timber, may bring one railing accusation against his school and college. Apart from mental discipline, the value of the ancient languages is to give a key to their literatures. Yet we make boys and young men spend ten or more years on the study of Greek and Latin, at the end of which time the beauties of the languages are still hidden because of the pernicious method in which they are taught. It passes my understanding how the more excellent way of Montaigne, of Milton, and of Locke should have been neglected until recently. Make the language an instrument to play with and to play with thoroughly, and recognize that except for the few in "Mods." and "Greats" it is superfluous to know how the instrument is constructed, or to dissect the neuro-muscular mechanism by which it is played. It is satisfactory to read that the Greek Curriculum Committee thinks "it is possible in a comparatively short time to acquire a really valuable knowledge of Greek, and to learn to read with accuracy and fair fluency some of the most important works in Greek literature." I am sure of it, if the teacher will go to school to Montaigne and feed fat against that old scoundrel Protagoras a well-earned grudge for inventing grammar—*pace* Mr. Livingstone, every chapter in whose two books appeal to me, except those on grammar, against which I have a medullary prejudice. I speak, of course, as a fool among the wise, and I am not pleading for the "Greats" men, but for the average man, whom to infect with the spirit of the Humanities is the greatest single gift in education. To you of the elect this is pure *camouflage*—the amateur talking to the experts; but there is another side upon which I feel something may be said by one whose best friends have been the old Humanists, and whose breviary is Plutarch, or rather Plutarch gallicized by Montaigne. Paraphrasing Mark Twain's comment upon Christian Science, the so-called Humanists have not enough Science, and Science sadly lacks the Humanities. This unhappy divorce, which should never have taken place, has been officially recognized in the two reports edited by Sir Frederic Kenyon,[8] which have stirred the pool, and cannot but be helpful. To have got constructive, anabolic action from representatives of interests so diverse is most encouraging. While all agree that neither in the public schools nor in the older universities are the conditions at present in keeping with the urgent scientific needs of the nation, the specific is not to be sought in endowments alone, but in the leaven which may work a much-needed change in both branches of knowledge.

---

[8] *Education, Scientific and Humane* (1917), and *Education, Secondary and University* (1919).

III

The School of *Literæ Humaniores* excites wonder in the extent and variety of the knowledge demanded, and there is everywhere evidence of the value placed upon the ancient models; but this wonder pales before the gasping astonishment at what is not there. Now and again a hint, a reference, a recognition, but the moving forces which have made the modern world are simply ignored. Yet they are all Hellenic, all part and parcel of the Humanities in the true sense, and all of prime importance in modern education. Twin berries on one stem, grievous damage has been done to both in regarding the Humanities and Science in any other light than complemental. Perhaps the anomalous position of science in our philosophical school is due to the necessary filtration, indeed the preservation, of our classical knowledge, through ecclesiastical channels. Of this the persistence of the Augustinian questions until late in the eighteenth century is an interesting indication. The moulder of Western Christianity had not much use for science, and the Greek spirit was stifled in the atmosphere of the Middle Ages. "Content to be deceived, to live in a twilight of fiction, under clouds of false witnesses, inventing according to convenience, and glad to welcome the forger and the cheat"—such, as Lord Acton somewhere says, were the Middle Ages. Strange, is it not? that one man alone, Roger Bacon, mastered his environment and had a modern outlook.[9]

The practical point for us here is that in the only school dealing with the philosophy of human thought, the sources of the new science that has made a new world are practically ignored. One gets even an impression of neglect

[9] How modern Bacon's outlook was may be judged from the following sentence: "Experimental science has three great prerogatives over all other sciences—it verifies conclusions by direct experiment, it discovers truths which they could never reach, and it investigates the secrets of nature and opens to us a knowledge of the past and of the future."

in the schools, or at any rate of scant treatment, of the Ionian philosophers, the very fathers of your fathers. Few "Greats" men, I fear, could tell why Hippocrates is a living force to-day, or why a modern scientific physician would feel more at home with Erasistratus and Herophilus at Alexandria, or with Galen at Pergamos, than at any period in our story up to, say, Harvey. Except as a delineator of character, what does the Oxford scholar know of Theophrastus, the founder of modern botany, and a living force to-day in one of the two departments of biology, and made accessible to English readers—perhaps indeed to Greek readers!—by Sir Arthur Hort?[10] Beggarly recognition or base indifference is meted out to the men whose minds have fertilized science in every department. The pulse of every student should beat faster as he reads the story of Archimedes, of Hero, of Aristarchus, names not even mentioned in the "Greats" papers in the past decade. Yet the methods of these men exorcised vagaries and superstitions from the human mind and pointed to a clear knowledge of the laws of nature. It is surprising that some wag among the examiners has never relieved the grave monotony of the papers by such peripatetic questions as "How long a gnat lives," "To how many fathoms' depth the sunlight penetrates the sea," and "What an oyster's soul is like"—questions which indicate whence the modern Lucian got his inspiration to chaff so successfully Boyle and the professors of Gresham College.

May I dwell upon two instances of shocking neglect? It really is amusing in Oxford to assert neglect of "the measurer of all Art and Science, whose is all that is best in the passing sublunary world," as Richard de Bury calls "the Prince of the Schooles." In Gulliver's voyage to Laputa he paid a visit to the little island of Glubbdubdrib, whose Governor, you remember, had an Endorian command over the spirits, such as Sir Oliver Lodge or Sir Arthur Conan Doyle might envy. When Aristotle and his commentators were summoned, to Gulliver's surprise they were strangers, for the reason that having so horribly misrepresented Aristotle's meaning to posterity, a consciousness of guilt and shame kept them far away from him in the lower world. Such shame, I fear, will make the shades of many classical dons of this university seek shelter with the commentators when they realize their neglect of one of the most fruitful of all the activities of the Master. In biology Aristotle speaks for the first time the language of modern science, and indeed he seems to have been first and foremost a biologist, and his

---

[10] Loeb Series.

natural history studies influenced profoundly his sociology, his psychology, and his philosophy in general. The beginner may be sent now to Professor D'Arcy Wentworth Thompson's Herbert Spencer Lecture, 1913, and he must be indeed a dull and muddy-mettled rascal whose imagination is not fired by the enthusiastic—yet true—picture of the founder of modern biology, whose language is our language, whose methods and problems are our own, the man who knew a thousand varied forms of life,—of plant, of bird, and animal,—their outward structure, their metamorphosis, their early development; who studied the problems of heredity, of sex, of nutrition, of growth, of adaptation, and of the struggle for existence.[11] And the senior student, if capable of appreciating a biological discovery, I advise to study the account by Johannes Müller[12] (himself a pioneer in anatomy) of his rediscovery of Aristotle's remarkable discovery of a special mode of reproduction in one of the species of sharks. For two thousand years the founder of the science of embryology had neither rival nor worthy follower. There is no reference, I believe, to the biological works in the *Literæ Humaniores* papers for the past ten years, yet they form the very foundations of discoveries that have turned our philosophies topsy-turvy.

Nothing reveals the unfortunate break in Humanities more clearly than the treatment of the greatest nature-poet in literature, a man who had "gazed on Nature's naked loveliness" unabashed, the man who united, as no one else has ever done, the "functions and temper and achievement of science and poetry" (Herford). The golden work of Lucretius is indeed recognized, and in Honour Moderations, Books I to III and V are set as one of seven alternatives in section D; and scattered through the "Greats" papers are set translations and snippets here and there; but anything like adequate consideration from the scientific side is to be sought in vain. Unmatched among the ancients or moderns is the vision by Lucretius of continuity in the workings of Nature—not less of *le silence éternel de ces espaces infinis* which so affrighted Pascal, than of "the long, limitless age of days, the age of all time that has gone by"—

> "... longa diei
> infinita ætas anteacti temporis omnis."

---

[11] Summarized from D'Arcy Wentworth Thompson.
[12] *Ueber den Glatten Hai des Aristotles.* (Berlin, 1842.)

And it is in a Latin poet that we find up-to-date views of the origin of the world and of the origin of man. The description of the wild discordant storm of atoms (Book V) which led to the birth of the world might be transferred verbatim to the accounts of Poincaré or of Arrhenius of the growth of new celestial bodies in the Milky Way. What an insight into primitive man and the beginnings of civilization! He might have been a contemporary and friend, and doubtless was a tutor, of Tylor. Book II, a manual of atomic physics with its marvellous conception of

> "... the flaring atom streams
> And torrents of her myriad universe,"

can only be read appreciatively by pupils of Roentgen or of J. J. Thomson. The ring theory of magnetism advanced in Book VI has been reproduced of late by Parsons, whose magnetons rotating as rings at high speed have the form and effect with which this disciple of Democritus clothes his magnetic physics.

And may I here enter a protest? Of love-philtres that produce insanity we may read the truth in a chapter of that most pleasant manual of erotology, the "Anatomy of Melancholy." Of insanity of any type that leaves a mind capable in lucid intervals of writing such verses as *"De Rerum Natura"* we know nothing. The sole value of the myth is its causal association with the poem of Tennyson. Only exsuccous dons who have never known the wiles and ways of the younger Aphrodite would take the intensity of the feeling in Book IV as witness to anything but an accident which may happen to the wisest of the wise, when enthralled by Vivien or some dark lady of the Sonnets!

In the School of *Literæ Humaniores* the studies are based on classical literature and on history, "but a large number of students approach philosophical study from other sides. Students of such subjects as mathematics, natural science, history, psychology, anthropology, or political economy become naturally interested in philosophy, and their needs are at present very imperfectly provided for in this university." This I quote from a Report to the Board of the Faculty of Arts made just before the war on a proposed new Honour School, the subject of which should be the principles of philosophy considered in their relation to the sciences.

That joint action of this kind should have been taken by the Boards of Arts and of Science indicates a widespread conviction that no man is cultivated up to the standard of his generation who has not an appreciation of how the greatest achievements of the human mind have been reached; and the practical question is how to introduce such studies into the course of liberal education, how to give the science school the leaven of an old philosophy, how to leaven the old philosophical school with the thoughts of science.[13]

It is important to recognize that there is nothing mysterious in the method of science, or apart from the ordinary routine of life. Science has been defined as the habit or faculty of observation. By such the child grows in knowledge, and in its daily exercise an adult lives and moves. Only a quantitative difference makes observation scientific—accuracy; in that way alone do we discover things as they really are. This is the essence of Plato's definition of science as "the discovery of things as they really are," whether in the heavens above, in the earth beneath, or in the observer himself. As a mental operation, the scientific method is equally applicable to deciphering a bit of Beneventan script, to the analysis of the evidence of the Commission on Coal-Mines, a study of the mechanism of the nose-dive, or of the colour-scheme in tiger-beetles. To observation and reasoned thought, the Greek added experiment, but never fully used it in biology, an instrument which has made science productive, and to which the modern world owes its civilization. Our every-day existence depends on the practical application of discoveries in pure science by men who had no other motives than a search for knowledge of Nature's laws, a disinterestedness which Burnet claims to be the distinctive gift of Hellas to humanity. With the discovery of induced currents Faraday had no thought of the dynamo. Crookes's tubes were a plaything until Roentgen turned them into practical use with the X-rays. Perkin had no thought of transforming chemical industry when he discovered aniline dyes. Priestley would have cursed the observation that an electrical charge produced nitrous acid had he foreseen that it would enable Germany to prolong the war, but he would have blessed the thought that it may make us independent of all outside sources for fertilizers.

---

[13] Since I wrote this lecture, Professor J. A. Stewart has sent me his just-published essay on *Oxford after the War and a Liberal Education*, in which he urges with all the weight of his learning and experience that the foundations of liberal education in Oxford should be "No Humane Letters without Natural Science and no Natural Science without Humane Letters."

The extraordinary development of modern science may be her undoing. Specialism, now a necessity, has fragmented the specialities themselves in a way that makes the outlook hazardous. The workers lose all sense of proportion in a maze of minutiæ. Everywhere men are in small coteries intensely absorbed in subjects of deep interest, but of very limited scope. Chemistry, a century ago an appanage of the Chair of Medicine or even of Divinity, has now a dozen departments, each with its laboratory and literature, sometimes its own society. Applying themselves early to research, young men get into backwaters far from the main stream. They quickly lose the sense of proportion, become hypercritical, and the smaller the field, the greater the tendency to megalocephaly. The study for fourteen years of the variations in the colour-scheme of the thirteen hundred species of tiger-beetles scattered over the earth may sterilize a man into a sticker of pins and a paster of labels; on the other hand, he may be a modern biologist whose interest is in the experimental modification of types, and in the mysterious insulation of hereditary characters from the environment. Only in one direction does the modern specialist acknowledge his debt to the dead languages. Men of science pay homage, as do no others, to the god of words whose magic power is nowhere so manifest as in the plastic language of Greece. The only visit many students pay to Parnassus is to get an intelligible label for a fact or form newly discovered. Turn the pages of such a dictionary of chemical terms as Morley and Muir, and you meet in close-set columns countless names unknown a decade ago, and unintelligible to the specialist in another department unless familiar with Greek, and as meaningless as the Arabic jargon in such mediæval collections as the "Synonyma" of Simon Januensis or the "Pandects" of Matheas Sylvaticus. As "Punch" put it the other day in a delightful poetical review of Professor West's volume:[14]

> "Botany relies on Latin ever since Linnæus' days;
> Biologic nomenclature draws on Greek in countless ways;
> While in Medicine it is obvious you can never take your oath
> What an ailment means exactly if you haven't studied both."

Let me give a couple of examples.

Within the narrow compass of the primitive cell from which all living beings originate, onomatomania runs riot. The process of mitosis has

---

[14] *The Value of the Classics.* Princeton University Press, 1917.

developed a special literature and language. Dealing not alone with the problems of heredity and of sex, but with the very dynamics of life, the mitotic complex is much more than a simple physiological process, and in the action and interaction of physical forces the cytologist hopes to find the key to the secret of life itself. And what a Grecian he has become! Listen to this account, which Aristotle would understand much better than most of us.

The karyogranulomes, not the idiogranulomes or microsomenstratum in the protoplasm of the spermatogonia, unite into the idiosphærosome, acrosoma of Lenhossék, a protean phase, as the idiosphærosome differentiates into an idiocryptosome and an idiocalyptosome, both surrounded by the idiosphærotheca, the archoplasmic vesicle; but the idioectosome disappears in the metamorphosis of the spermatid into a sphere, the idiophtharosome. The separation of the calyptosome from the cryptosome antedates the transformation of the idiosphærotheca into the spermiocalyptrotheca.[15]

Or take a more practical if less Cratylean example. In our precious cabbage-patches the holometabolous insecta are the hosts of parasitic polyembryonic hymenoptera, upon the prevalence of which rests the psychic and somatic stamina of our fellow countrymen; for the larvæ of *Pieris brassicæ*, vulgarly cabbage butterfly, are parasitiased by the *Apantales glomeratus*, which in turn has a hyperparasite, the *Mesochorus pallidus*. It is tragic to think that the fate of a plant, the dietetic and pharmaceutical virtues of which have been so extolled by Cato, and upon which two of my Plinean colleagues of uncertain date, Chrysippus and Dieuches, wrote monographs—it fills one with terror to think that a crop so dear to Hodge (*et veris cymata!* the Brussels sprouts of Columella) should depend on the deposition in the ovum of the Pieris of another polyembryonic egg. The cytoplasm or oöplasm of this forms a trophoamnion and develops into a polygerminal mass, a spherical morula, from which in turn develop a hundred or more larvæ, which immediately proceed to eat up everything in and of the body of their host. Only in this way does Nature preserve the Selenas, the Leas, and the Crambes, so dear to Cato and so necessary for the sustenance of our hard-working, brawny-armed Brasserii.

---

[15] Of course I have made this up out of a recent number of the *American Journal of Anatomy*, 24, I.

From over-specialization scientific men are in a more parlous state than are the Humanists from neglect of classical tradition. The salvation of science lies in a recognition of a new philosophy—the *scientia scientiarum* of which Plato speaks. "Now when all these studies reach the point of intercommunion and connection with one another and come to be considered in their mutual affinities, then, I think, and not till then, will the pursuit of them have a value." Upon this synthetic process I hesitate to dwell; since, like Dr. Johnson's friend, Oliver Edwards, I have never succeeded in mastering philosophy—cheerfulness was always breaking in.

In the proposed Honour School the principles of philosophy are to be dealt with in relation to the sciences, and by the introduction of literary and historical studies, which George Sarton advocates so warmly as the new Humanism,[16] the student will gain a knowledge of the evolution of modern scientific thought. But to limit the history to the modern period—Kepler to the present time is suggested—would be a grave error. The scientific student should go to the sources and in some way be taught the connection of Democritus with Dalton, of Archimedes with Kelvin, of Aristarchus with Newton, of Galen with John Hunter, and of Plato and Aristotle with them all. And the glories of Greek science should be opened in a sympathetic way to "Greats" men. Under new regulations at the public schools, a boy of sixteen or seventeen should have enough science to appreciate the position of Theophrastus in botany, and perhaps himself construct Hero's fountain. Science will take a totally different position in this country when the knowledge of its advances is the possession of all educated men. The time, too, is ripe for the Bodleian to become a *studium generale*, with ten or more departments, each in charge of a special sub-librarian. When the beautiful rooms, over the portals of which are the mocking blue and gold inscriptions, are once more alive with students, the task of teaching subjects on historical lines will be greatly lightened. What has been done with the Music-Room, and with the Science-Room through the liberality of Dr. and Mrs. Singer, should be done for classics, history, literature, theology, etc., each section in charge of a sub-librarian who will be *Doctor perplexorum* alike to professor, don, and undergraduate.

---

[16] *Popular Science Monthly*, September, 1918, and *Scientia*, XXIII, 3.

I wish time had permitted me to sketch even briefly the story of the evolution of science in this old seat of learning. A fortunate opportunity enables you to see two phases in its evolution. Through the kind permission of several of the colleges, particularly Christ Church, Merton, St. John's, and Oriel, and with the coöperation of the Curators of the Bodleian and Dr. Cowley, Mr. R. T. Gunther, of Magdalen College, has arranged a loan exhibition of the early scientific instruments and manuscripts. A series of quadrants and astrolabes show how Arabian instruments, themselves retaining much of the older Greek models, have translated Alexandrian science into the Western world. Some were constructed for the latitude of Oxford, and one was associated with our astronomer-poet Chaucer.

For the first time the instruments and works of the early members of the Merton School of astronomer-physicians have been brought together. They belong to a group of men of the fourteenth century—Reed, Aschenden, Simon Bredon, Merle, Richard of Wallingford, and others—whose labours made Oxford the leading scientific university of the world.

Little remains of the scientific apparatus of the early period of the Royal Society, but through the kindness of the Dean and Governing Body of Christ Church, the entire contents of the cabinet of philosophical apparatus of the Earl of Orrery, who flourished some thirty years after the foundation of the Society, is on exhibit, and the actual astronomical model, the "Orrery," made for him and called after his name.[17]

---

[17] Among other notable exhibits there are:

    1. A series of astronomical volvelles in manuscripts and printed books.

    2. The printed evidence that Leonard Digges of University College was the inventor of the telescope many years before Galileo.

    3. The mathematical work of Robert Recorde of All Souls' College, in which he suggested the St. Andrew's Cross as the sign of multiplication, and uses symbols +, -, =.

    4. The earliest known slide-rule in a circular form, recently discovered in St. John's College.

The story of the free cities of Greece shows how a love of the higher and brighter things in life may thrive in a democracy. Whether such love may develop in a civilization based on a philosophy of force is the present problem of the Western world. To-day there are doubts, even thoughts of despair, but neither man nor nation is to be judged by the behaviour in a paroxysm of delirium. Lavoisier perished in the Revolution, and the Archbishop of Paris was butchered at the altar by the Commune, yet France was not wrecked; and Russia may survive the starvation of such scholars as Danielevski and Smirnov, and the massacre of Botkin. To have intelligent freemen of the Greek type with a stake in the State (not mere chattels from whose daily life the shadow of the workhouse never lifts), to have the men and women who could love the light put in surroundings in which the light may reach them, to encourage in all a sense of brotherhood reaching the standard of the Good Samaritan—surely the realization in a democracy of such reasonable ambitions should be compatible with the control by science of the forces of nature for the common good, and a love of all that is best in religion, in art, and in literature.

Amid the smoke and squalor of a modern industrial city, after the bread-and-butter struggle of the day, "the Discobolus has no gospel." Our puritanized culture has been known to call the Antinous vulgar. Copies of these two statues, you may remember, Samuel Butler found stored away in the lumber-room of the Natural History Museum, Montreal, with skins, plants, snakes, and insects, and in their midst, stuffing an owl, sat "the brother-in-law of the haberdasher of Mr. Spurgeon." Against the old man who thus blasphemed beauty, Butler broke into those memorable verses with the refrain "O God! O Montreal!"

Let us not be discouraged. The direction of our vision is everything, and after weltering four years in chaos poor stricken humanity still nurses the unconquerable hope of an ideal state "whose citizens are happy ... absolutely wise, all of them brave, just, and self-controlled ... all at peace and unity and in the enjoyment of legality, equality, liberty, and all other

5. The early vellum and wooden telescopes of the Orrery Collection.

6. An original Marshall microscope.

7. Early surveying instruments, including the great quadrate of Schissler.

good things." Lucian's winning picture of this "Universal Happiness" might have been sketched by a Round Table pen or some youthful secretary to the League of Nations. That such hope persists is a witness to the power of ideals to captivate the mind and the reality may be nearer than any of us dare dream. If survived, a terrible infection, such as confluent smallpox, seems to benefit the general health. Perhaps such an attack through which we have passed may benefit the body cosmic. After discussing the various forms of government, Plato concludes that "States are as the men are, they grow out of human characters,"[18] and then, as the dream-republic approached completion, he realized that after all the true State is within, of which each one of us is the founder, and patterned on an ideal the existence of which matters not a whit. Is not the need of this individual reconstruction the Greek message to modern democracy? And with it is blended the note of individual service to the community on which Professor Gilbert Murray has so wisely dwelt.

With the hot blasts of hate still on our cheeks, it may seem a mockery to speak of this as the saving asset in our future; but is it not the very marrow of the teaching in which we have been brought up? At last the gospel of the right to live, and the right to live healthy, happy lives, has sunk deep into the hearts of the people; and before the war, so great was the work of science in preventing untimely death that the day of Isaiah seemed at hand, when a man's life should be "more precious than fine gold, even a man than the golden wedge of Ophir." There is a sentence in the writings of the Father of Medicine upon which all commentators have lingered, "ἢν γὰρ παρῇ φιλανθρωπίη, πάρεστι καὶ φιλοτεχνίη"[19]—the love of humanity associated with the love of his craft!—philanthropia and philotechnia—the joy of working joined in each one to a true love of his brother. Memorable sentence indeed! in which for the first time was coined the magic word "philanthropy," and conveying the subtle suggestion that perhaps in this combination the longings of humanity may find their solution, and Wisdom—*Philosophia*—at last be justified of her children.

THE END

---

[18] *Republic*, Book VIII.
[19] *Œuvres complètes d'Hippocrates*. Par E. Littré, IX, 258.

www.ingramcontent.com/pod-product-compliance
Lightning Source LLC
LaVergne TN
LVHW091528170726
843492LV00004B/1113